BLUFF YOUR WAY
IN
GOLF

PETER GAMMOND

D1137238

RR
RAVETTE BOOKS

Published by Ravette Books Limited
3 Glenside Estate, Star Road
Partridge Green, Horsham,
West Sussex RHl3 8RA
(0403) 710392

First printed 1985
Reprinted 1987,1988,1991,1992

Series Editor - Anne Tauté

Cover design - Jim Wire
Printing & Binding - Cox & Wyman Ltd.
Production - Oval Projects Ltd.

The Bluffer's Guides are based on
an original idea by Peter Wolfe.

CONTENTS

Clobber
Clothes 12
Clubs 13
Balls 16

Actually Playing It 18
The Hold-in-One 21
Putting 22
Par or Scratch Score 23

Rules 24
Cheating 26

Societies 28

Golf Courses 30
An Interlude 32
Clubs 33
The Match 35

Golf Players 38
Golfing Types 40
Alf 43
Professionals 47

Handicaps 48

Golf Humour and Literature 51

A Purple Patch 54

Glossary 55

INTRODUCTION

Golf, it should be stated right away, is no laughing matter!

For those who become involved in it, professionally or otherwise, it is a very serious business indeed. Lives and homes are ruined by it. Golf is habit-forming and can have a serious effect on your health.

If golf is your *modus bluffi*, however, you need never go to a party or dinner in fear of finding nobody to talk to. There is always someone who

a) plays golf and needs a shoulder to weep on,
b) plays golf and may be about to give it up,
c) used to play golf but has given it up because of an incurable slice or a third divorce;
   or, best of all,
d) is just about to take it up. The ideal victim. You may even be able to sell him your old golf clubs.

Those who are able to take an objective view may well scoff. But never those who are drawn into the web of its fatal fascinations.

Quite apart from the havoc caused to married life, the golfer is a frustrated creature who spends life wrestling with the challenge of imposing the well-nigh impossible upon the improbable. The battle is hardly ever won.

The only thing that can be said in Golf's favour is that it gives plenty of scope to practised bluffers. Before playing the game they can compile a fictitious air of assurance and knowledge that can completely destroy their opponent's confidence: 'Did a ten-over-par last time I was out here. Nasty second half, though!' Whilst actually playing, the bluffer may bluff everyone with a series of devices which we shall be discussing more fully later. Particularly himself.

Afterwards, as the bitter memories fade and the alcohol begins to have its benevolent effect (all true golfers drink), they can indulge in that form of bluffing that is better categorized as 'the distorted memory'; and actually return home glowing in several colours. This does not alleviate the loved one's suffering in the least.

'Must you go off and play that wretched game again, darling? Leaving me here, alone and sad, to slave over the microwave oven?'

'Yes, I must, I have promised to make up a four.'

'Have you no regard for our marriage? Mother did warn me about golfers, but I never thought it could be like this.'

'You are being very selfish. I must keep fit. And in any case the Club Trophy is next month and I am very out of practice.'

'One day you will return to find me gone, the house empty, the children on the streets.'

'Yes, well I must be going now. If we don't get off by two, it gets very crowded. I'll be back in time for supper.'

And off she goes to the Club and he returns to the kitchen. It is a sad little scene that is repeated, with variations, the world over, every day.

CLOBBER

There are two extreme views on what you require to play golf. It is universally agreed that you must have some clubs and a ball – the question of how many clubs, and which, is a much-discussed and erudite subject – but even before you get to handling a club there are two important considerations:

1. What to carry the clubs around in.
2. What to wear while using them.

The positive approach is to go all out to impress by having the biggest, best and most outrageous of all these things. This obviously puts a less well-equipped golfer at a great psychological disadvantage – quite apart from being distracted by it all.

The other extreme is to carry a light bag with a minimum of clubs. Some of the very best golfers do this and find it an effective ruse. They tend to be the youngish and athletic ones and always carry the bag over their shoulder. Always be wary of people with a small ancient bag and a minimum of clubs – quite possibly hickory shafted. They could be bluffing, of course, but it is just possible that they may have discovered the secret.

Many golfers take a middle course and simply carry what they really need, but these generally turn out to be middling golfers who are continually out-smarted by the others.

Those who will be 'helping' you take your first faltering steps into Golf, notably the club professional and his accomplices, will unquestionably favour the positive approach. Likewise the manager of the sports emporium if you choose to purchase your goods from this source. Although the club professional is probably the greater salesman of the two and will undoubtedly get you to buy more, it is probably best to get most of your things from him in the first place as this will entitle you to be greeted by him on your future visits to the Club and, better still, for you to be on 'Good-morning, George' terms. This obviously makes an impression on any guests you may have with you. Later you may surreptitiously buy your balls from mail-order firms at half the price, so long as you occasionally buy one or two from George, cheerily explaining that you don't appear to be losing so many lately.

Bags

The first thing that you are expected to get is a golf-bag, and every effort will be made to persuade you to buy the biggest available. This could be an enormous leather contraption which, in addition to space for clubs, has numerous zippered pockets all over it making it roughly the same shape and size as Tessie O'Shea. Try not to get carried away. Unless you are the kind and class of golfer who regularly employs a caddie you are going to be bearing the load. Bags of this kind are mainly intended for your wardrobe. The pockets reduce in size until number thirty or so is a tiny thing with a cute little zip in which to carry a pencil or a thermometer. There is never any guidebook to your golf-bag available. In years to come you may find that you have been carrying around in some remote recess half-a-bottle of whisky, a family of fieldmice and several pairs of decaying gloves.

Spares

What to put in your expansive and expensive container? First of all, the clothes which you will not actually be wearing but may need to wear. These are mainly various so-called waterproofs. You really require about three lots: a light set for summer showers; a medium set for average rainfall; a heavy-duty set for winter blizzards. None of these ever actually keep the wet out. The secret has either never been discovered or, you may suspect, remains intentionally undiscovered so that you will keep on buying new sets of garments in fond hope. You should therefore always carry a towel, preferably two; a small one to dry yourself and a bigger one to dry your clubs.

Hats

Not one, but a variety of hats is essential. A brightly coloured one with a long peak, adjustable for size by means of an inefficient sort of contraption at the back, which will make you look like Gary Player or Lee Trevino. You can touch it with the same mock deference as they do whenever you manage to sink a problematic putt.

A woolly cap with a bobble on the top of it. Make sure the bobble is very bobbly, loosely attached and large so that you can bobble it just as your opponent is about to play. If you are going to have such a hat, it might as well be a sizzling colour. A sober one is going to be much less effective.

The man who does not wear a hat with a bobble on it is probably the man who does not need a hat with a bobble on it. Even dispensing with the bobble but keeping the hat may suggest a degree of confidence that most will not possess.

There is no reason why you should not also carry a fur hat for extreme conditions – except that they tend to fall off during the swing. A variety of caps may be added with various densities of check pattern according to where you are playing.

Umbrellas

Your bag will have fittings to carry an umbrella. Golfing umbrellas, as even the non-golfer will know, are huge and generally made up of panels of contrasting primary colours. The only reason for this is, once again, distraction. A dull umbrella would be much less effective a weapon even if put up at vital moments or seen bowling along the fairway in a high wind. Nowadays it is perfectly possible to get umbrellas, if you know the right people, with advertising slogans on them like 'Buy a Volvo' or 'Drink Pepsi-Cola'. There is nothing more effective when standing near an opponent deeply snared in a bunker than these aggravating slogans. There is never any time when he is less likely to be in want of a car or a coke. So a garish umbrella of this kind would be ideal. No golfer would be seen dead with such an object away from a golf course, or wearing a bobble hat for that matter; but on the golf course normal human behaviour is not expected.

Etceteras

For extreme weather conditions, a good skin-cream and items of eye-protection equipment ranging from sunglasses to snow-goggles should be carried. The golfer with imagination and a feeling for self-preservation will find many things essential to his peace of mind. For instance, a thermometer, a barometer, wind and rain gauges and a compass. One must always bear in mind the possibility of getting lost in the rough, when it would be best to be prepared with a bottle of something sustaining and some basic rations. Army survival packs are ideal for this sort of emergency. Perhaps a lightweight tent and some sort of signalling device like a Verey pistol or a small foghorn.

The thorough golfer will also carry a small library,

including a guide to the best golf courses; detailed maps of the course actually being played with distances marked; a good-pub guide; the Book of Rules; spare scorecards, a little pad with a clip to put them in, and several pencils (as these are always going astray); and a pocket dictionary of colloquial phrases and terms of abuse.

If you attempted to carry your portable canteen yourself you would be too exhausted to play and possibly permanently disfigured. You will therefore either have to have a caddie or some sort of device on which to put it in order to get it round the course. A golf-trolley is essential to the normal person. Nowadays, most clubs insist on a trolley with wide wheels which make it much heavier to pull. You may therefore be tempted to purchase an electric trolley. Not many British clubs either encourage or allow those things they have in America which actually carry the golfer as well, unless it's for the the disabled or the Club Captain or the Secretary. Most of today's golf-trolleys remain permanently attached to the bag and fold up so that they can be put into the car boot. A small hoisting device might be of some assistance at this point.

The older golfer may like to take a small folding seat along and a kidney machine.

While you're about it, you might as well add one or two other things. Like a telescopic contraption for retrieving balls out of water. Many golfers now have these and one we know has long ago made his pay for itself by charging 5p to his erstwhile friends for each ball retrieved. At the same time he manages to pick up several more balls, given up by other players, and is thus never short of them. Recently, at a local club, a small pond was drained for cleaning and over three thousand golf balls were taken from its muddy depths. The golf ball business is a good one to be in.

And in case one of those awful days comes when you arrive at the course to find a notice saying NO TROLLEYS, you should always be sure to have a light bag that will carry the two or three clubs actually necessary to play.

Clothes

Now we have dispensed with spare clobber, there are the essentials. Golf is about the only game in the world where people, particularly in the summer, put on more clothes to play than they would normally wear. The man who has been pottering round in his garden in a pair of shorts because of the heat, will dress up in order to play golf. The Club Rules require it. There has been an observable tendency of late for younger players and those who have nice knees to wear shorts, even in the British Isles. It is, of course, common practice in warmer climes. Here it is still done with a sense of guilt. Stern notices appear on the club notice-boards: 'Shorts are permitted but long stockings must be worn and the shorts must be of decent length'.

Provided you are reasonably dressed in oldish clothes the rules of Golf do not make any further demands. But custom has it that you wear clothes of tweedish aspect and garish colouring. Men and women who are quite normal members of the Conservative Association at home and in the street, appear in light blues, pink, spots and checks, plus-fours, funny hats, sun visors, and black-and-white shoes, looking something like a 1925 dance-band crooner. Any old sweater would do for golf but the majority wear special golf sweaters which have a well-known trademark or the name of a notorious golfer emblazoned upon them and which cost three times as much as the same articles without.

12

The golfing glove is also a thing of many colours – all unpleasant. You only buy one of these, which at least saves a considerable sum of money. It is supposed to help your grip. Most players take them off and stick them in their back pockets when putting. Most golfers would play just as well without a glove, particularly when it gets wet.

As for shoes: a lightweight summer pair is needed for the occasional fine day; and a normal leather pair with spikes; and some hopefully waterproof ones for wet weather. Only golf shoes which cost a hundred pounds or more are even remotely damp resistant.

So you are now sartorially equipped and you have a bag full to the brim with life-saving equipment. Now you come to the mechanics of the business and brace yourself to purchase a set of clubs.

Clubs

No club professional or golf shop proprietor would agree, but all that is needed to play a good round of golf is a putter, a sand-wedge, a 5-iron – and a ball. Most amateurs would play a better round with just a 5-iron than they do with all the clubs in the world.

The rules of Golf state that not more than fourteen clubs may be carried. The golf bluffer usually carries exactly fourteen. He is thus one up on the man who only carries thirteen, or six up on the man who only carries eight and so on. On the other hand, he could be considered to be ten down on the person who only carries four *and* plays better golf.

Some wise golfers have discovered for themselves that there is hardly any effective difference between a reasonably cheap set of clubs and a very expensive one. They will not be seduced by talk of carbon shafts and steel heads. The average golfer is convinced, however, that only the very best is really good enough for him.

13

You really do not need a full set of clubs. No amateur golfer uses even half of the weighty lot that he lugs around to impress his golfing friends. If you walked around carrying just the minimum number mentioned above, plus, perhaps, a wood of some sort, tied together with an elastic band, you would probably gain quite a reputation. Unfortunately most golf clubs insist that you go out with a bagful per person. Their main concern is to make the golf shop a profitable concern so that the pro will stay with them.

If you don't want to buy a full set of clubs you might find some broken ones around the course: you could use just the tops of these to fill up the empty spaces in your golf-bag.

Irons

But let us suppose that you have a complete set. These should include a group with metal heads, called irons, and nowadays numbered from 1 to 9. The lower the number the straighter the face. As no golfer with a handicap over 10 can hit anything with **Nos. 1-3** without either driving the ball into the ground or paralysing his hands, you should regard **No. 4** as being the one for having a distant go with. Just keep Nos. 1-3 slightly soiled so that they look as if they have been used. An average golfer will have one club somewhere between 4 and 6 which he uses for almost everything; the 5 being the great favourite which sells better than any other number. With this, by accident or intent, you may hit a high looping shot, a straight low one, or even putt onto the green in fair weather.

The **No. 7** is used when you are quite near the green but not near enough to use a **9**. Nobody uses an **8** except by mistake. You will gather that the higher numbers are used for the shorter shots. If the golfer has a consistent swing, he will achieve various calculable diminishing distances from 1-9. The good golfer says to his caddie, 'A 7 do you think', and the caddie says:

Golf Story . . . the caddie says 'Well, I advised the Club Captain to use an 8 from here yesterday.' So the golfer uses his 8 but gets nowhere near the green. Golfer to caddie: 'I thought you said you told the Captain to use an 8 here yesterday?' Caddie: 'Yes. He didn't reach the green either!'

As the average golfer does not have a consistent swing he is likely to loft a 5 and top a 9 and thus get the same distance with both. (When you top a ball it is because you have lifted your head to look at a golfer of the opposite sex and have hit the ball on the upper edge, either burying it in the ground or sending it bounding along at daisy-level. You loft it when you are trying too hard to get it up in the air and you hit right underneath it.) Many golfers have an even more sloping club called a sand-iron or sand-wedge, which is really meant, as the name implies, for use in bunkers, but is often used by the pros for short shots off the fairway. When the amateur golfer does this the ball usually goes straight up in the air and lands at his feet.

Woods

Then we come to the woods. These have longer shafts and knobbly wooden heads. They are used to hit the ball off the tee and for long shots off the fairway. Professionals use the **No. 1** or 'driver' but amateurs are better advised to start off with a **2** or a **3** if they are to get anywhere at all. Being longer-shafted and generally more flexible the woods tend to give the player more length than an iron. On the other hand they are much less accurate and there is an even greater likelihood of missing the ball altogether. Lots of pros use irons off the tee and it is considered quite a clever thing to do; in fact some commentators go so far as to say 'I really thought he would have taken an iron there.'

But an amateur who uses an iron off the tee is considered to be chicken, incompetent or geriatric. This means a ready line of patter must be to hand if you are playing so badly at the moment that you daren't use your woods.

'Nearly always take an iron here, you know. Nasty cross-wind. Did you see Faldo hit that beauty on the television yesterday – 16th wasn't it? Do you mind moving back a bit there.'

All this is in preparation for a rather feeble thrash with a 5-iron that does little beyond adding a superfluous stroke to the score.

In more romantic days irons and woods used to have descriptive Anglo-Saxon names like 'mashie', 'cleek' and 'spoon' (see **Glossary**). It is a great asset to be able to use these with conviction and mystifies everyone in this mathematical age.

Do not forget: no set of golf clubs is complete without a matching set of covers to go on the woods. Some fairly practical but dull ones can be bought in the golf shop, but this is where one of the family can be really useful by knitting a set in brightly coloured wool – with bobbles on. A really practised bluffer can get several bobbles in action at the same time.

Balls

The original golf ball was a spherical bag made of leather which was then stuffed tight with boiled feathers and made as nearly round as this primitive form would allow. Mishaps with this kind of ball were frequent and many a game ended in a shower of feathers which soon dispersed in those uniquely changeable winds that blow over golf courses – always into the face of the player in whichever direction he happens to be going.

The next kind of ball was made of rubbery substance called gutta-percha which, when heated, could be rolled into ball-shape and then hardened. They were known as gutties. And were very popular.

At this point the Americans took over golf. So it was an American who invented the modern golf ball with a soft core round which yards of elastic were wound and the whole then covered with an outer sheath of gutta percha. The gutty school strongly opposed this but had to give in eventually when the undoubted superiority of the new ball allowed their opponents to win with expensive inevitability. Up to 1921 golf balls were made in various sizes and weights but that year the Royal and Ancient and its American equivalent decided on a regulation ball whose weight was not greater than 1.62 ounces and whose diameter was not less than 1.62 inches.

The Americans soon got tired of being like everyone else and decided that their balls ought to be bigger than everyone else's. So they increased the official size to 1.68 inches. As the Americans were better at the game than anyone else, the rest of the world eventually had to agree to adopt the new size although the controversy over whether it was best to have big or little balls raged for a long time.

The only advance since then is the cheap Japanese ball which is made of one-piece solid material and which often breaks into pieces when hit, each bit flying off in a different direction with a savage buzzing noise. The biggest piece is the one that counts.

ACTUALLY PLAYING IT

The theory, as any golfer will tell you, is very simple. Starting with the club-head near the ball, you slowly bring it back behind the head and if you swing it down on exactly the same course, whacko! – there you are. All you have to do for this success is to make sure your feet are correctly placed in relation to the ball, that you are gripping the club properly, that your arms and elbows move through certain prescribed trajectories, that the whole body moves smoothly so that there is no snatching or jerking of the club and it comes to the ball in an even, accelerating arc and, after striking, continues over the left shoulder in what is called the follow-through. Oh, and you should be perfectly balanced through all this and your eye should be kept firmly on the ball, head down and un-moving. So you see there are difficulties. The average person, for instance, is not naturally adept at keeping his head still while all the rest of him is in violent action. Most of us (which is why few become successful pianists or drive a car well) are only able to do one thing properly at a time. Remembering to do and/or not to do seven or eight things all together and in the space of half a second is difficult, even impossible. Nor does it help to have several people watching you attempt this feat – all of them (with the possible exception of your playing partner) hoping that you will make a botch of it. Bad golfers are only truly happy when they have got away from everyone else and are able to take what they consider to be their natural easy swing at the ball.

So why not follow the natural easy swing method? After all lots of people can hit a nail on the head with a hammer. The trouble is that while you are being natural you tend to forget the inbuilt disadvantages of being splay-footed, pot-bellied, short-sighted and generally unbalanced. While instinctively compensating for these disabilities you forget to keep your elbows in, to grip the handle firmly, etc. etc., and the club does not come down the same way as it went up.

At this point, or very soon after, the average golfer loses his cool and he decides to have a go at it. He slashes wildly at the ball with great force – and it sails over the adjacent main-line railway or lands in a pond. There is a basic rule to all ball games. If you try to hit a ball hard it goes nowhere in particular. If it is struck smoothly, sweetly (and, with surprisingly little effort) it will go a long, long way.

The second basic rule of Golf is 'never despair'. There is always somebody who is worse than you are. Sometimes you may find this hard to believe, but it is a fact. If you can find such a person then play with him or her – as an opponent, of course, not as a partner. The truth is that golf is far more a matter of applied psychology than a matter of physical ability. If you can actually manage to win a hole then it goes without saying that your morale will be high. You will, however, almost inevitably play the next hole badly and things will slump. But never be foolish enough to play with someone who is a lot better than you are, even on a friendly basis. Some say you should. In tennis, or some game where it is a matter of being in direct opposition, playing somebody better can often lift your game, even in defeat. But in golf, where it is all up to you, it is courting disaster. The more you try to match their long hits, the shorter and more desperately wayward yours become. If you are the worst player in a foursome you can become a depressive maniac in no time at all as you constantly trudge along behind, in a desperate course, from one bunker to the next while the other three chat merrily about their talents and the excellent shots just made.

The amateur game is roughly based on the professional one — but only roughly. The professional game, when all is going well, is simply a matter of mathematical calculation. A professional (and a low-handicapped amateur), always assumes that he is going to hit the ball perfectly and therefore golf is, to him, only a matter of taking the right club. 'The distance', says the caddie, 'is 135 yards. Therefore a 7 iron is required and, as the green is slightly tilted to the rear, a degree of backspin will be required. Oh, and also a little fade to the right to allow for the wind'. The bluffing golfer will of course try to give a similar impression. Ah, yes a 7 he says aloud to himself, but I think today as the air is a little heavy that I will use a 5. Backspin did you say. Ah, yes — and a little fade to the right. His ensuing shot which sends the ball off to the left and, being also topped, rather low in trajectory, may well scramble through a bunker, hit a bump and land quite near the green. 'I was afraid of going over the green so I used the bunker to slow it up' one golfer was heard to say.

That is the sort of thinking that goes on in the head of an average golfer. Very rarely does he achieve that frame of mind where he thinks he is going to put it right by the flag. If he did there is every chance that he would. More likely his troubled mind is saying: 'As it's a downhill lie I am sure to top it and it will end up in that bunker. I am therefore going to play safe and try a gentle lob into the middle of the green, steering clear of both bunkers in case it should turn out to be a low one.' He tops it and it scuttles through the green, hits a rake which someone has left at the back and rebounds to within six feet of the pin. The player hastily puts the 9 iron back in his bag and says, as the others come up, 'I thought the low approach was the sensible one in these conditions'.

NB: Don't be awed by rank once you are out on the course. Captains, for example, are often chosen for their social rather than their golfing assets. Always play with a Captain in the afternoon. They are often quite erratic but most of them even more so after they have been in for lunch and been treated to a round or two. Club secretaries are nearly always indifferent golfers but difficult to play against as you don't really want to beat them. Ordinary club professionals are sometimes worse than you'd expect.

The only way to play golf well is to go out with a clear conscience and a clear head. Never speculate about the game. Concentrate on each shot but don't start thinking you are going to do a good round. That way disaster lies. If you can induce a completely 'don't care' sort of mood you may end up playing well. But it is hard to achieve.

The Hole-in-One

The most poetical moment in Golf is the Hole-in-One. As the ball goes, usually in an erratic and unexpected way, or after some incredible bounce and hitting the flag, into the hole on the usually intractible Par 3, the observers (and there must be observers or it doesn't count) will either say 'Bravo!' (immediately thinking of the inbuilt drawback – see below) or 'What a fluke!' But they are the mean sort; the mean average golfer.

The inbuilt drawback for the golfer, though many are so delighted that they think it worth it, is that, by an old custom, you have to buy drinks for everyone in the club house. This can be expensive. It is possible that many Holes-in-One go unrecorded except on the heavenly scorecard. It follows that the best time to have a Hole-in-One is sometime like early in the morning, playing with two reliable teetotal witnesses. Get back to the club house before the lunchtime lot begin to arrive.

Anyway it doesn't happen to many.

Putting

Apart from the few arrogant, low-handicapped individuals who are good at all parts of the game, golfers are mainly divided into two groups:

1) those who are reasonably good at getting to the green but can't putt for toffee
2) those who have difficulty in getting to the green but feel happy once they have reached the smooth-cropped surfaces.

Those who are in the second group are never able to see why so many golfers get het up over the simple matter of putting. But if you have got onto a green in, let us say, 4, then you have a burning desire to get the ball down in only one putt. This induces a state of nervous anxiety and all sorts of twitches. To have got all that way in 4 and then to take another 3 shots over the common, seaside pastime of putting is apt to ruin your scores and your pleasure. The second kind of golfer on the other hand, having taken 6 to get to the same green, has got over all his nervous tensions in the rough and the bunkers and now feels positively light-hearted. He will often find no difficulty in getting the ball in the hole with one deft putt and, to the annoyance of the twitcher will have halved the hole with him. So it is the better golfer who so often gets in a tangle with his putting, adopting all sorts of strange crouches like one afflicted with rheumatics, or getting all twisted up like that chap from Notre Dame. Some will grip their putter a foot from the base; some hold it vertical, some hold it between their legs. The incurable twitch is awful to see. The poor fellow draws the putter back smoothly enough but as it goes toward the ball the head stops in the middle of the stroke or twists to one side. Overcome by the thought that he is going to miss the hole, he does.

The happy kind, on the other hand, has the feeling that he is going to get it down and he does. Before all golfers looms the spectre of the hapless pro who, before a million eyes missed a short putt and lost a major championship. It would be unnecessarily cruel even to mention the name of Doug Sanders, so we won't.

Par or Scratch Score

The Par laid down for any given golf course being something of a grail far beyond the reach of any average golfer, is always a bone of contention. The discontent is mainly manifested on individual holes – usually what the player refers to as a 'bloody long par 4' i.e. a green which he is supposed to reach in 2 strokes but will only do so on miraculous occasions with a strong following wind and drought conditions.

All club committees, even of the most lowly of clubs, like to imagine that their courses will frequently be used by Jack Nicklaus and Ballasteros who might well get onto a par 5 in two strokes, and rate them accordingly. The average golfer will on the average get onto a par 4 in 3 (two good hits and a chip) and, in order to achieve his par, will have to get down in one putt. It makes it very hard work and eternally frustrating. His delight when he gets a birdie – i.e. one less than the par for the hole, is therefore extreme and he will talk about it for days afterwards with a fervour that is only matched by his description of the one that eluded him through no possible fault of his own – bad bounce, sudden gust of wind, opponent talking, etc.

All bogies (any score over par) are theoretically described as 'should have been a par', likewise all pars as 'should have been a birdie'; and even birdies (may they be forgiven) as 'should have been an eagle' (two under par), despite the fact that an eagle is something they have never achieved in a lifetime of playing.

23

RULES

No game has more rules than Golf. It is an essential part of the bluffer's equipment not so much to know them all as to know which it is necessary to know, together with a handful of irrelevant ones to trot out on telling occasions. It was found in the days when the golf-rules were few and simple that there was nothing to be gained by knowing them because everyone did. The ruling body of Golf therefore set up a special team of experts to expand the rules of golf as rapidly, and in as complicated a manner, as they possibly could. The team works hard at this year in year out and the Rule Book gets bigger and more incomprehensible all the time. Particularly the bits about handicapping and scoring.

It is a good thing to carry an older book of rules than the current one. Few will ever query its date. The fact that it is a book of rules is sufficient. For that matter you could write your own and few would know the difference. All golfers stand in awe of the rules. Particularly those with money on the game. But they always do their best to bend them. Some (though we hesitate to admit this) actually cheat!

There is a subtle line drawn between Rules and Etiquette. There are numerous official regulations about what the player can do on the tee; but it is the Etiquette bit at the end of the book that says: *'No one should move, talk, stand close to or directly behind the ball or the hole when the player is addressing the ball or making a stroke.'* You can, however, cough or sneeze or smoke a pipe and send dense clouds of smoke before the player's eyes. You could even sing an operatic aria (which is not specifically forbidden). Many of those waiting to go off regularly sigh deeply and are not penalised.

Here are a few interesting rules that may be trotted out at odd times:

'If the ball oscillates without leaving its original position it has not moved.' ... 'Your ball moved then!' 'No it didn't, it only oscillated!' 'What do you mean, oscillated?'

'During the play of a round the player is responsible for the actions of his caddie'. ... 'I say, your caddie moved then, do control him.' 'No he didn't, old boy, he only oscillated!' 'What do you mean, oscillated?'

'A caddie is deemed a "loose impediment".'

'If the ball in motion be stopped or deflected by any outside agency, it is a rub of the green and the ball shall be played as it lies, without penalty.' ... 'Sir, you hit my caddie!' ... 'He is a loose impediment.' ... 'He was only oscillating.' ... 'He was making casual water.' ... etc.

The rule writers get quite concerned about some things – *hazards* for example. Hazards are, after all, the things that make golf exciting – flying balls, swinging clubs and what not. But it is the fight against nature about which the rulemakers wax lyrical. *'Interference by casual water, ground under repair, or a hole, cast or runway made by a burrowing animal, a reptile or a bird'* is what worries them a lot. If a ball coming up against one of these is not visible *'the player may probe for it'*. On the other hand if he is about to step into some water up to his waist, he must not *'test the condition of the hazard or of any similar hazard'*. You'd think they would at least let him put his elbow in it to see if it was too cold. Or send the caddie in first to see if there are any reptiles about. In any case *'in order to treat the ball as lost in the hazard, there must be reasonable evidence that the ball lodged therein'*. If it has been swallowed by a reptile living in the hazard there is not much you can do about it, and the rule makers are not at all helpful. They will pursue a point so far but no further.

25

Cheating

Cheating has been known in golf. Not, we hasten to add, by us personally or anyone that we know and play with. Nor is the cheating of serious proportions. Just a little manipulation, sometimes accidental. But it does happen.

Cheating off the tee is rather difficult, at least on the part of the player as he is being watched rather closely. It is more likely the opponent who will cheat if you should care to call it that, by a well-timed cough or dropping a club. Some blatantly talk, but this can, of course, be stopped by a sharp look. The only eventuality that must be taken into account is that of missing the ball altogether – what is technically termed an 'airshot' and counts as a stroke if you are playing strictly by the rules. Many superior opponents will achieve a point by overlooking it. But in case the worst should happen you should always have a preliminary practice swing so that everyone gets used to the idea. It would then be ideal if your real swing also had the appearance of being a practice swing so that your unconcern registered better. However, the trouble is that a swing that looked like a practice swing but was a real one would turn out worse than a genuine practice swing which is usually a better one anyway than the real one that it precedes. You could end up with a bit of a pig's ear.

Once down the fairway, the chances for a little manipulation increase. In fact the worse your shot (and subsequently your probable distance from the other players) the more you can do. In winter or bad conditions the player is allowed to *roll* i.e. move the ball a short distance if it is in a hole or somewhere he doesn't like very much. You should therefore always roll as a matter of principle until someone says 'Hey . . . there's no rolling'. You can then innocently apologise.

The ploy of not being certain that it is your ball is a common one. Turning it to see whether it has 'Property of the Westwich Driving Range' written on it, or perhaps even a maker's name, you may be able to move it ever so slightly to a better position. This works especially well in the short rough. The fact that you know perfectly well that it is your ball need not deter you. The rules of golf are so strict that should you not check and should you by chance play someone else's ball, you would be heavily penalised.

If the ball has landed in the real rough, then provided you have got there before anyone else, some slight adjustment of the lie is almost beyond resisting. The decent bluffer would not do anything untoward (i.e. toward the hole) but others might. Loose dead twigs may be moved away. How unfortunate if it should move the ball a little. Very unscrupulous players, we suspect, might even have another ball handy so that it can be dropped in a better position. That sort of thing happens to James Bond and we all know how suggestive films can be.

The bunker is an absolute must for a little gentle deception. Not only because of those forbidding walls of sand and grassy overhangs, but mainly because, in a bunker, you must not 'ground' the club. That is to say, it must not touch the sand before you have played your stroke, though it may hit the sand first *during* the stroke.

On the green manoeuvres are minimal. You are, of course, allowed to pick up the ball to clean it and a few inches may be gained this way. Always put the marker down in front of the ball but replace the ball in front of the marker. Even most professionals do this as the action is not usually closely watched. Never be lured by a patronising: 'Would you mind putting your ball down out of the way. Save you marking it'. It is a well known saying that a putt taken in haste is oft repented. That's what your opponent hopes. On the other hand you stand to gain a lot by preferring to mark an eighteen-inch putt knowing that this will leave the opponent with a four-footer in a state of uncertainty. Well-meaning but over-loud cries of 'Do you want the flag out or tended?' can easily disrupt concentration. Most telling of all, the apparently friendly 'Tricky length that' or 'Quite a bit of golf there yet'. Putting is entirely in the mind. On a bad day even the best can be persuaded to miss.

SOCIETIES

Groups of golfers who, tired of playing with Alf, Bryan and Ron, form themselves into a society (with Alf, Bryan and Ron as a nucleus) in order to organise, say, four matches a year played on various courses. They are often based on professions or trades, such as the Yarmouth Pork Butchers Golfing Society, the String Maker's Guild Golfing Society, the Professional Hang-men's Golfing Society – and so on. Societies are welcomed by most Golf Clubs, as they provide an easy rake-off, always being charged more than ordinary players. But they are not liked by the members of the Club they are visiting (like Alf, Bryan and Ron) because it upsets their weekly game.

The Society is tirelessly organised by a Secretary who seems to get some sort of masochistic pleasure out of it as he will have done it for at least ten years, at the end of which he will be thanked by the current Captain and get a round of applause and an inscribed salver. He has to try, though without much conviction, to get everyone out on their allotted time, in groups of three or four.

Everyone plays worse than they usually do on their own well-beloved courses and it rains for at least two out of the four matches played in any year. Leaving their ill-marked, often soggy, scoring cards with the Secretary and his long-suffering assistant the golfers change into sporty blazers and society ties. After drinks there is a perfunctory dinner from which the golf club tries to make as much profit as possible, and then comes the Prize-Giving. The first prize is generally won by a visiting guest so he is given the golf umbrella while the Cup, a rose-bowl encrusted with crossed niblicks, goes to steady old Ron who has won by dint of never driving more than a hundred yards and never going off the fairway. There is a remaindered barbecue set for Bryan and a set of tartan moleskin club covers for whoever it was that came third. And some indefinable object for the best over-85 score. And a wooden spoon for Alf.

Then there is the raffle, insincere thanks are rendered to all and sundry, and off they all go, back to their butchering, stringing and hanging, leaving the make-believe golf match world behind.

The golf bluffer is in his element in these Society affairs. Pleased to be moving in society, he gets further joy from having his handicap reduced, as many societies insist on a minimum allowance. He can therefore bask in being 20 for a day even though it may ruin his winning chances. There is a great general confusion over handicaps anyway and many bluffs are made and called. The air is alive with stories of what various players have achieved elsewhere on their own courses or at other meetings they have attended. Unlike today when they were slightly off form. The winners can hardly believe their luck. Those who go home to their loved ones have their final bluff of the day in an unspoken suggestion that the six balls they won in the raffle at a cost of £5 were, in fact, some sort of prize that made the whole day worthwhile.

GOLF COURSES

The idea of the golf course is that it is a great trial of strength and character. One of the great adventures of life. Mentioned in the same tones that men speak of the battlefields of two world wars – the Somme, Ypres, El Alamein, the Arakan. It is a justified comparison. Hear the players drone on: 'It was on the Burma Road (i.e. the West Course at Wentworth, Surrey) that I got one of my best pars. On the 7th I think. Par 4 as you know, 403 yards. Nearly went into the heather at the bottom. Hit an almighty 8 iron. Bounced off a tree and landed right on the green. Could easily have been a birdie but it just curled round the hole.'

'Ah, yes, reminds me of the Royal at Lytham. Playing up the 2nd, I get a bit of a slice and the ball goes out toward the railway line. Thought I'd lost it but it hit the rails and bounced right back into the middle of the fairway. 11th's the worst hole I've played though. Blind shot off the tee and bunkers like trenches. Took 9 there.'

'What about the 17th on the Old Course at Walton Heath . . .?'

'Not as bad as the 17th at Hoylake.'

'Does it compare with the 14th at Moor Park?'

'What about the 11th at the Royal North Devon? I went into the rushes there and it took me nine to get out.'

'If you get into the bunker at the 3rd at St. Enodoc it's all you can do to climb up to the ball, let alone hit it . . .'

And so it goes on. For those who still carry the scars of those hard-fought campaigns, each heartfelt stroke is imprinted deep in the memory.

You must accept the fact (however difficult it is to believe it) that golf courses are actually planned by people known as golf course designers. It is not nice to have to contemplate the depths of cunning, treachery and general ruthlessness that must prompt such a person or persons to inflict so much anguish on those who, by the very nature of their impulses, are as sensitive and as easily wounded as golfers.

Imagine two such characters who have been asked to turn a bit of blasted heath or shaggy woodland into a golf course. Listen, if you care to, to their tortuous thoughts as they pick their untroubled way through mire and gorse.

. . . That would make a splendid opening. Nothing like a dip to make distance difficult to assess. We'll leave the boggy bit at the bottom. Nice dog-leg next. They won't know about that quarry until they come round the corner . . .

Now there's a nice long stretch for a par five. That'll instil a feeling of hopelessness. A shorty here, I think. Some of them are bound to go over the back and into that tangle of briars. Nice tilt on the fairway there to throw them into the trees. Curved one next. They're sure to try to cut the corner and if we leave that pine there 60 per cent will hit it. Look! A pond full of lilies. What about a short one over that, with a green sloping back toward the water and the flag right on the edge? Dredge it every month and the club will make a nice profit in balls. A nasty deep ditch across this fairway. A bottomless bog beyond. No warnings. Just a 'ground under repair' sign. They're bound to ignore it. Now a good uphill climb. Hole will always be known as 'Old Coronary'. What better than a narrow passage through trees to end with, and the final green right in front of the club-house. Insure the windows heavily.

You still think the 12th was a bit too straightforward? Never mind. Give them one to raise their hopes. In any case we can keep the rough pretty long. Fancy a game of golf next week? No thanks, gave it up years ago. . .

AN INTERLUDE
(overheard on the radio)

Chairman: Alan – which would you pick as your particular favourite?

A: Oh, I think without doubt the 5th. Difficult to approach in many ways, and it has come in for a lot of criticism. Many go astray on that last difficult stretch – but what satisfaction when it comes just right.

C: Peter?

P: I agree, basically, but I think I still prefer the 9th. A good rhythm is essential here if we are to avoid the many traps. But once those are negotiated the trouble-free serenity of the run-in is magnificent.

C: John?

J: I still think of the 1st as setting the pattern of the rest. Not seeing the final objective adds a lot to the challenge here. Right away we're amongst the trees as it were.

A: Yes, but it is often a bit heavy going. Almost too much of a challenge too early.

P: It is odd that we all pick the odd numbers. 4, 6 and 8 all have contrasting attractions. Less demanding perhaps but plenty of hazards.

J: I always remember the first time I met up with the 8th during the war. Immediately you felt that you had to get right into the heart of things. A couple of deft and perfectly timed strokes could do it.

C: So far we have only discussed the early sequence. Don't you think that after the 9th, the more complicated twists and turns add a new dimension to our enjoyment?

A: Of course. The massive 11th in particular poses unique problems. But so satisfying to overcome them. Even when you have reached the target it is difficult to hold. It can fall away at the end if we are not careful.

P: And by the time we reach the harrowing 13th the impetus may have gone. Our attention can often wander at this point.

J: And yet the ever enigmatic 15th always leaves us thirsting for more.

C: Well, thank you gentlemen. I hope we have set the scene for some fascinating performances this week. Peter, as one who has known all of these on many occasions, what do you predict? A final word.

P: I think it is going to be a fascinating experience.

C: Thank you Alan, Peter, John and thank you at home for listening. The broadcasts of the complete cycle of Shostakovich symphonies will be heard each night for the next fortnight. We'll be back 'Talking Music' next week at the same time.

CLUBS

Not the sort one plays with but the kind you belong to.

The top-class golf clubs (including most of those with 'Royal' attached to their name) take this Club business more seriously than it is taken in any other sport, except perhaps Cricket. They model themselves on exclusive gentlemen's clubs in London and like to have a few leather chairs scattered round the place as a reminder. Such clubs are, of course, very particular about who goes in them. Simply being pricey is today no bar to any unsuitable person coming in as a guest; although it is easy enough to get him debarred as a member. The atmosphere at some of these holy of holies is not far removed from a cathedral. The nervous or humble golfer is never quite sure whether he ought not to take his shoes off on entering. The presence at the bar of assorted Who's Who candidates and a formidable bristle of brigadiers is enough to intimidate even the boldest of bluffers.

Don't be put down. It is rather like asking someone to step onto the stage of the National Theatre without warning, and deliver the soliloquy from *Hamlet,* but you must enter these clubs with a bold demeanour and talk in as loud a voice as you can muster. Dress, of course, is tremendously important. Golf clubs are obsessed with dress. While a suit, in a sporting establishment would be a bit ridiculous, there is no doubt that a well-cut blazer and dark grey flannel trousers with expensive shoes are standard form. A tie suggestive of some sporting prowess is a great help. It may only be that of some minor Oxford or Cambridge college but most people will confuse it with something more important. The best clubs do not allow people to drink in comfortable clothes at the bar. Open-necked shirts – that sort of thing – are absolutely taboo. The incredibly

33

expensive golf apparel that you have been so pressingly persuaded to buy is only for outdoors.

The most experienced golfers can be thrown off balance by a top-class Club whose members know how to make them feel ill-at-ease and unwelcome. You can never be sure at first of the pecking order, or power, of the hierarchy. In some clubs even the barman has to be spoken to with a degree of humble respect, especially if he also turns out to be the club steward. 'No sir, I'm afraid we don't serve that kind of thing in here,' he may say, and you are not sure whether he is referring to your order for a port-and-lemon or to your brother-in-law.

Club secretaries vary enormously in effect. Those of the bluffing fraternity may have established a position of extraordinary power and influence. Some have been heard to address members who have committed some minor infringement on the course in a way that would get them a punch on the nose anywhere outside a golf club. It is, on the whole, a good thing to be on christian name terms with the Secretary.

But the people who really run the Club are, of course, the Committee, with whom you must either be on equal terms, or forever remain on the fringe. It is not merely enough to know them. Someone you may have known for years and played golf with and talked to in tones of amiable familiarity on the 'Hi, John' level, once on the Committee has to be spoken to with careful deference. 'Good-morning, John' at least, but not even that until he has said 'Good-morning' to you. Knowing the Captain is a tremendous coup, but to know the Mafia behind him who are in a string-pulling position is really something to aim for.

Nor does it stop there, for if you are not quick to assert your superiority you will find yourself being quite humble to green-keepers (particularly head ones) and even the Club professional.

The aim of all golfers is to be fully accredited seven-day members with committee service behind them and the captaincy theirs for the asking. The fact that the best that can be achieved is a nodding acquaintance with the assistant barman and a handicap of around fifteen should not blunt your aspirations.

All of which applies to the ladies' section of any Club, although there, we understand, the class distinctions are even more rigorously observed.

There is a legendary assumption (carefully nurtured by those in financial circles) that belonging to a golf club, and thus mingling with potential associates and customers, is a desirable thing. Some banks and building societies, for example, actually encourage their managers to play golf every day – and only those who don't like playing it are likely to object. Some of these take this so seriously that many of their employees are unaware of their tenure. Unpleasant though it is to undermine old tradition, it must be said in the cause of truth, that no-one has ever conducted or acquired any business on a golf course or in a golf club. They are much too busy discussing their swing or their putting-twitch. Either that, or they are too full of alcohol to be interested in anything remotely resembling business.

So far, we have been discussing the higher-class clubs, those whose premises resemble, and indeed were, the country seat of a bankrupt Earl and whose course is simply a deer-park without the deer. To get into one of these is a matter of persistent graft and stamina. If you are one of the leathery-skinned, heavy-drinking, quizzical, battle-scarred, fearless sort who led their men into action with a cry of 'tally-ho' you may have no difficulties. Otherwise you will. The top-class American clubs, unable to compete with the title 'Royal' and a clientele of decayed gentry, simply go for the money angle. Their best clubs are modelled more on four-star country hotels where he who has a ready supply of greenbacks is made to feel good and wanted. They are the kind of clubs that supply every man or woman's need from a pink gin to a hand of bridge, which is why all serious American golfers want to get into a select few of ours.

Needless to say, all clubs are not able to attain these high levels. The middle-range do their best by maintaining similar rank and file relationships and plastering the club-house with petty rules and regulations on the scale of a seaside boarding-house. The best of them have their club-houses situated a decent distance from the actual battleground. Second best clubs have a habit of having their custom-made members' bar window overlooking the first tee. This is a particularly nasty ploy and brings one back to the harsh reality that most golf clubs, whatever their social priorities, do expect their members to be able to play the game.

However, all that really matters in this situation is that you get off the first tee in a respectable manner and out of sight of the regular members and the Membership Committee. How you achieve this is your business. Nobody can help. But to fail and to find yourself taking your second shot a mere five yards or so from the club-house, and the third, maybe, from an adjacent bush, is the most humbling of all human experiences.

At the bottom end of the scale there are the plainest of clubs which are pleased to admit anyone of whatever prowess and class. Here those genteel souls whose only real failing is that they can't play golf and are not allowed even to try at the weekend are forced to rub shoulders with artisan golfers. And only the golf itself makes that bearable.

THE MATCH

Most of the golfer's life (and his money) is spent in preparation for the great day – the golf match. The day when he feels sure that he will triumph over adversity and at least win a packet of three golf balls of a kind he doesn't ever use.

A golf match is designed to make as many people as possible unhappy. Not just one or two as in most sports, not even eleven or fifteen – but perhaps as many as seventy people at a time (which is about the size of golf society that the average golf club can't quite cope with). At the end of it all, only one of that band of hopefuls has any claim to be contented. But even they, in the clubhouse afterwards, will be bemoaning the fact that they just failed to better their previous best score. Or that they just missed the hole-in-one by a matter of millimetres.

Those who come in second are the saddest of all. It is never their fault that they put the ball into the water at the 15th. Their hopes have been narrowly shattered and they have once more missed the golden opportunity of taking that dreadful set of cut-glass home. The third-placed are hardly less unhappy having won yet another striped umbrella to add to the six they already have in the garage.

The organisers are unhappy as some rather nasty criticisms have been levelled at them. The Club officials are unhappy. They always are. Even the Club cat is unhappy as, with so many people around, there is nowhere to sit. Perhaps they who come in seventieth and earn the coveted wooden-spoon of Troy are the happiest. At least they know they can never be in a worse position.

Everyone vows to give up the game for ever. Then they have another drink – and start discussing the next meeting.

GOLF PLAYERS

There has been curiously little written about the golf mentality. Plenty about its techniques and appurtenances, its courses and its star players, but practically nothing about its motivations and its correlative attitudes. If you can simply spring something like *that* on a golf conversation, you will be in a strong position. The bluffer who actually digs into golf in a Freudian sort of way is going to prove a devastating opponent amongst those whose basis of conversation is simply the size of their balls, the line of their swing and the unmentionable things they did on the 15th last Thursday.

So first, **motivation and correlative attitudes** or in other words, what it is that makes people play golf – and the psychological and domestic upsets that are the inevitable outcome.

What can one compare with the position of the fallible golfer (and that includes most professionals and accomplished weekenders as well as neurosis-ridden five-dayers) who, standing on the first tee in a state of pessimistic expectancy, surrounded by hostile interest, with rain assailing his being, sets out to hit a small hard ball with an ill-conceived appliance towards a hole that is so distant as to be well nigh invisible to ageing optics, or possibly not even in sight at all?

There is a fifty-fifty chance that the ball will be lost in some distant hazard, but he doesn't really care about that. All he wishes, fervently, is that its destination shall be distant. If it is 'straight down the middle' – fine; it is manly or golfing-womanly to hit a long shot, even if it is never seen again. It is a sign of debilitation (cf. *Oxford Dictionary* 'having a feeble constitution further weakened by a dissipated life, 1871', which could also be deemed an accurate description of the average golfer) to hit something feebly or not at all.

It may therefore be assumed that golfers play golf to prove that they can mentally overcome the pressures that golf puts upon them. The fact that if they didn't play golf at all they would not have to endure or overcome its pressures may not occur to them.

So what gets them out there in the first place? Goodstein's argument that golfers are getting away from their marital partner is well supported by the fact that 99 per cent of golfers are married. One rarely meets an unmarried one. There is also social status: the Club aspect of golf still has a residual hold on the golf scene. It continues to be considered a gentlemanly sport – in spite of cumulative evidence to the contrary. Although indulged in by such extreme beings as ploughmen and peers, it still has a solidly middle-class feel about it. But the average amateur has often taken to golf because he is no longer fit enough to play the active games of his youth like soccer and squash, or even those of his first signs of decline like tennis and jogging. The only place where the average golfer breaks into a trot is between the 18th green and the club-house. If he ran he would never make it.

Golfers are mainly debilitated (see above) and most have already had a good go at further weakening their constitutions. It is clear, therefore, that one of the reasons for playing golf is to be able to claim indulgence in sport and fresh air. Playing a sport and breathing air in spite of an increasing girth, poor eyesight, dicky heart, varicose veins and blood pressure is a defiant gesture by those whose lives are otherwise devoted to concentrated dissipation and indulgence. Murchison's theory that golf is a monosexual sport may have some validity, but it fades into insignificance beside our theory of physical inadequacy.

Golfing Types

You are either a golfer or you are not. There is no halfway mark. Just as with alcoholics, gamblers and freemasons, a commitment to golf must be total. That is why it is played by such a strange race of men and women.

Some sorts of people the average golfer will never actually meet, let alone play with. They will be seen playing in matches. The curious thing is that all the best club players, in golf or tennis, or what-have-you, never seem to practise. They just appear in matches with their low handicaps and swipe things well down the fairway. The young, fit and arrogant golfers don't play with average golfers. They could all be professionals if they wanted, but they don't care to. They don't hang about in bars much. They wear shades of perfectly-fitting yellow and green that you wouldn't care to be seen in and look bronzed and lithe. To be spoken to by a good player is worth several strokes in your own game.

That golf is a mental game as much as a physical one, at least at the average level, is borne out by the proficiency or lack of it exhibited by various occupational types. Doctors, barristers and other professional men generally seem to be pretty good at it and hover around the 10 mark. They treat golf as they treat their clients with a sort of disdainful superiority. They are not the sort of people to let golf get the upper hand. Bank and building society managers, though they play six or seven times a week, can be good at the game but they have their off days, probably coinciding with days when the pound has fallen or they have mislaid something. Artistic types fluctuate even more. Actors (particularly comedians) often have low handicaps which are usually a more accurate reflection of their inventive powers than their golf.

Engineers, builders and owners of demolition businesses generally have a bull-headed approach which stems from their occupations. If you get it right – jolly good. If you get it wrong, well, that's life. Retailers and market-gardeners tend to have a steady, down-the-middle sort of attitude. They don't hit things far but they keep to the fairway, and often put in good Stableford scores as a result.

The Short, Fat and Rounded. Many variations of small plump men and women (*knolls*) play golf. Lacking the midriff flexibility of the young and lean they develop highly personal styles. The short back swing is the most usual. This, in the hands of some professionals (and indeed amateurs) can be effective and accurate but it rarely achieves length and can lead to other defects like snatching. The small round golfer is frequently aggressive.

The Long and Lean. Can manage a fuller swing but tend to use contorted poses to save having to stretch for the ball. Can be great hookers and slicers.

The Stickler. The one who has read and knows the rules. All of them. A menace to play with as he is constantly on the lookout for any infringement. Likes to point them out at crucial moments.

The Know-All. The sworn enemy of the bluffer. Tends to know about the technicalities of Golf – or at least thinks he does. Frequently around to tell you what you should do in bunkers and ponds. Displays no great aptitude in these situations himself but is always ready to instruct others. The trick is to ask him if he would mind stepping back fifty yards or so as you keep seeing him out of the corner of your eye. He will take this badly and, with luck, may not speak to you again.

The Slow and Steady. Usually middle-aged and after. Has learned over the years that there is no sense in taking a whack at the ball. Having repeated 'slow and steady' to himself countless times over the years he has at last become so slow and steady that one occasionally wonders if he has solidified.

The Chatterbox. One of the worst to play with although he may be a very nice chap and the life and soul of a party. But the incessant flow makes golf almost impossible.

The Rogue. The one who thinks that all that matters is to win. He frequently likes to play for money as well. It therefore pleases him, for he has no pride or bigheadedness about him, to play off a high handicap. It allows him to win tournaments *and* his sidebets. The rogue is, of course, greatly disliked by everyone and deemed a 'pirate'. The only reason he does not beat everyone by this sly means is that most of the people he plays with are 'pirates' too.

The Sport. Youngish sort. Takes golfing holidays in Portugal; plays squash, badminton, tennis; possibly even jogs. Has a good-looking young wife who does aerobics. Often carries his golf-bag with just a few efficient-looking clubs in it. Frequent first remark: 'Haven't played for six weeks'. Then proceeds to hit long, accurate shots and scores in a carefree manner. Don't play with this one if you can possibly help it.

The Good Sort. In case we seem to be loading things rather heavily against the golfer, there is also the nice golfer (Honest Stan), who rabbits away uncomplainingly, is naively delighted when he does a good shot; and even (mark you) expresses admiration when *other* people achieve good things. The Stans of the golfing world are truly rare.

Alf

An Alf is an essential item in anyone's golfing life. As the best way to bluff your way through a round of golf is to play with someone who is guaranteed to be more erratic than you are, there is a great demand for the company of an Alf. Your Alf might be called Percival or John or Zez – but, for the moment let's stick with Alf.

Alfs always have the hidden capacity to be quite good players. Our particular Alf is a soundly built fellow and has the strength to hit the ball for miles. He is, we might add, generally a very equable, helpful and friendly chap away from the golf course. Occasionally he achieves a full-blooded, well-directed swing and the ball goes a long, long way. These shots he generally plays with his eyes apparently closed. He has even been known to achieve a birdie and his simple elation on these occasions is heart-warming to behold. One is always pleased when Alf wins a hole.

Unfortunately these triumphs always have a sort of Jekyll-and-Hyde effect on him. He seems to forget that he is Alf and would happily answer to the name of Gary, Arnold or Jack. He now believes he is going to carry all before him. The next drive he delivers with a wild ferocity and power that makes everyone around step back a pace or two. Shoulders hunched he really means to hit that ball. Should he actually make contact it may go an even greater distance than before but in such a wild variety of directions that the only sensible place to stand is well behind him – though even that is not a guarantee of safety.

The ultimate destination of these shots is indicated by a rising of rooks among the trees, a distant splash, the sound of breaking glass or cries of anger and anguish from an adjacent fairway. Alf, who is a great reader of books upon golf, explains in a few terse technical terms to the momentarily silent spectators that he was not properly lined up (which they could see anyway) or that something slipped.

Even more often, the ball scuttles for a few yards along the ground or, keeping very low, buries itself in the back of some nearby eminence.

To give a particular instance; recently Alf drove his first tee-shot into a bunker. It happened to be a bunker on the nearby 9th and a group completing their first half displayed signs of antipathy to this muscling in on their hole. It took him three shots to get out of the bunker so deeply had the ball embedded itself, and another two to get a hundred yards down the fairway. After this his morale was understandably low and he was not responding well to the jovial comments of his companions. It took him several holes to recover his bonhommie. Alf is always worrying about how many *over* five he is at each point of the course. He doesn't often have to think in terms of being *under*. Having scored about 45 on the first five holes he is apt to get depressed. Sometimes even violent. One feels that it would be better if he didn't dwell on the score so much: away from the golf course he is such a gentle sort of chap.

Alf is the only golfer who has been seen to lose five balls on the first tee. This happened at one of those very upper-class Surrey golf courses much frequented by retired Generals and Managing Directors having what they describe later as a business lunch. Now Alf is never slapdash in his approach to golf. Whereas chaps like Trevino just step up to the ball and wang it down the fairway, Alf prepares for his drive with great thoroughness. He shuffles his feet almost as much as Fred Astaire, then aligns his bottom and indulges in fifteen or so preliminary waggles of the club. He then takes off his glasses and cleans them, then goes through the routine again. This particular day he went through this rigmarole as usual and the half-a-dozen or so fours waiting to go off behind him were clearly impressed and expected something good after such a thorough preparation. The average General has himself got to his high position in life by proper attention to detail.

The first four lost balls were simply a matter of that golfer's disease, excusably prevalent on the first tee, known as topping. Each of them went into the adjacent areas of the thick and well-nigh impenetrable heather and gorse that are a picturesque feature of this particular course. A concerted effort by everyone around (including an ex-Chief Inspector of Police) failed to reveal their whereabouts. As, judging by the increasing violence of the blows they had been dealt, they were probably a yard or so beneath the surface of the sandy sub-soil, this was not surprising.

The ever-growing assembly of top brass behind, though definitely interested, were beginning to get a bit restive, but generously agreed that Alf should have another go. In fact, they were probably intrigued to see what might happen and were utilising the ego-boosting effect of watching somebody who was doing worse than they could possibly dream of. They were not disappointed. Alf next achieved something that is rarely seen. Professional golfers can impart a fair amount of backspin with a wedge, but Alf achieved the same effect with his driver. His club went so low and hard under the ball, imparting the finest of touches to its underside (presumably known as bottoming, though we haven't come across the word) that it acquired a phenomenal amount of backspin. While Alf stared with a puzzled expression down the fairway, the ball actually went backwards, buzzing like an angry bee, through the ranks and upper ranks of the waiting golfers. This was not taken too well though all agreed that it was unusual. In fact it aroused a considerable amount of discussion as it was a situation which nobody could remember having seen covered in the Book of Rules. It was finally decided by a Committee member that, as Alf's ball was now on the 18th fairway, all those waiting to go off the 1st were entitled to do so (and hopefully get well clear) before he played his next shot.

So it was some twenty minutes later before Alf next went into action. Those who were with him were all for giving up and going for a drink, but Alf's enthusiasm was still high. In a slightly petulant mood, he refused to indulge in any half measures like playing a safe shot with an iron. Fortunately he now hit a powerful, zooming, immensely long shot (as he is wont to do on unexpected occasions) which went straight into a rarely used bunker some two hundred yards or so down the left of the fairway. This made him even more militant. Stepping into the bunker, he forewent his usual preparations and hacked at the ball with a wedge and with immense bottled-up ferocity. It flew screaming out of the sand, very high and surprisingly far, soaring over a line of trees and out of bounds into an adjacent swimming-pool belonging to a television celebrity who lived in that salubrious area. He was in it at the time. The ball didn't actually hit him and his protests seemed quite excessive for someone so reliant on a good public image.

Alf was firmly persuaded not to go and ask for his ball back and was allowed a free drop.

Golf is never dull when you are playing with an Alf. For that matter, golf is rarely dull at any time. Maddening, sickening, frustrating, hateful, yes, but rarely dull.

Professionals

One of the finest things about golf is that the veriest amateur is allowed to play on the same courses as the most hallowed professional. One day he may be rabbiting around and ruining the fairway, and the next day he may watch Tom Watson in the same spot, taking out even greater divots, though this time intentionally.

If he can afford to go and watch the professional contests he will not be seated about a mile away from the players as in other sports. He will be able to stand right beside these bronzed heroes, and even chat with them. Arnold Palmer once asked our advice about a shot at Wentworth, took it, and missed the hole by miles.

You may not be able to get your own swing right but you are perfectly entitled to criticise Lee Trevino's which, as any book will tell you, is all wrong.

The big difference between the professional and the amateur is that the pro probably gets up early before a match and goes out and plays a few hundred practice drives, approach shots and putts. His play is akin to that of an advanced robot. When things go wrong it is only because a spectator has moved, a camera flashed, or a distant hawk has batted an eyelid. Or because of a bad bounce. It happened to you last week in the same place and you could have told him if only he'd asked.

Ah, what feats of endeavour down the ages, Hogan and Hagen, Henry Cotton – plus-foured and invincible, Bobby Locke, Gene Saracen. To the casual observer all they did was hit a ball a long way with grace, nonchalance and purpose. To those who play golf they were all miracles, heroes; they knew the secret that occasionally we know, when there is that sweet sound and you are on the distant green in two, and down in a single putt. It is almost a shame for the pros that they do this sort of thing all the time. It must get tedious.

HANDICAPS

One of the best features of golf, and one that holds the most possibilities for the serious student of bluffing, is one that has little to do with the actual playing. We refer to the Handicapping System – or Scheme as it is officially, and candidly, called.

In simple terms, handicapping is introduced so that an average or poor player can enjoy a game of golf on something like an equal footing with the very best, even a Scratch, player. This somewhat abrasive-sounding term is applied to a player who is deemed capable of going round a course where the par is said to be 72 in 72 strokes. All professionals are euphemistically classified as Scratch players. The average player might find that his average score week after week is round about 98 – more or less. He would then be deemed a player with a 26 handicap. So theoretically if Tony Jacklin and one of us played our local course together, he would score 72 and we would score 98 and the game would be a draw. Actually he would probably score 69 and we, playing in a state of acute nerves in his presence would score 117. But that is beside the point.

The amateur player's handicap is based on score cards that he has submitted after playing in an official club or society match. Not those which he has filled in when playing with his drinking friends or by himself or dreamed about. As few people ever play as well in a match as they do in a friendly game, being all tensed up for the occasion, there is a tendency for handicaps to be rated a little on the high side.

The matter is complicated, however, by the fact that there are two sorts of golfers – an honest minority and a dishonest majority. The honest minority try to have a handicap that reflects their true ability and will see that it is adjusted if they are playing well. You may never meet one of these but they do exist, mostly in the form of committee members who have to be careful.

The handicap system causes most bitterness in society matches where everyone suspects everyone else. The only person who is generally liked is, remarkably, Alf or his equivalent. The lowest imaginable handicap for a club member is set at 28 (Category 4 golfers are 21 to 28 handicap) so the rabbit whose real handicap would be about 50 is never going to diddle anybody.

The English Golf Union, who like to keep up the pretence that golf is a nice, clean, gentlemanly and thoroughly honourable game are naturally concerned to see that the handicapping system is not abused. They therefore lay down strict rules for the submission of cards. Like all authorities they are incapable of phrasing their rules in language that anyone like a Category 4 golfer can understand. For some unfathomable reason they decided at the beginning of 1983 that all players should have two handicaps: *'an Exact Handicap'* and *'a Playing Handicap (Definition G)'*. The Exact Handicap is recorded to one decimal place which, when rounded to the nearest whole number (0.5 upwards), gives the Playing Handicap from which the player competes.

This is fine in principle but they tend to go on and say things like 'If a player plays above his Playing Handicap or records a "no return" his Exact Handicap is increased by an amount determined by the Category of his handicap *but not determined by the extent to which he was above his* Playing Handicap.' Furthermore: 'The recording of scores shall be kept by Nett Differential *i.e. the difference (+ or −) between the player's nett score and the Standard Scratch Score.*' However many times one reads that sort of thing, the essential truth at the core of it seems to slip away and the average player is inclined to say 'let's not bother about strokes today. We're all much the same.'

Very rarely, when asked before a match what his handicap is, will a player simply say 26 or 10 and leave it at that. He will say 'Well actually I am 26 . . .' which carries the implication that he is more like 20 (which may well be true in good double bluffing tradition); or he might say 'I play off 26' which somehow suggests that he is actually about 32 but is forced to conform to a 26 handicap accrued one golden day.

On the other hand both statements might imply the exact opposite, according to whether the golfer looks one in the eye or not. The lower the handicap the more likely it is that the player will be pleading his own cause. 'I play off 10' suggests a degree of doubt in the player's mind and a probable ability of about 16. No golfer in that sort of category is likely to say he is 10 when he is really 4. He just could not bring himself to do so. What he is more likely to say (truthfully or not) is 'Well I used to play off 4 but nowadays more like 10'. 'Are you saying you *are* 10?' his opponent asks. 'That is my present playing handicap' he will reply, and the opponent is now left in a nice state of doubt as to whether to expect golf of a 4 or 10 handicap standard. It will probably be 16.

The phrase 'Well they have given me a handicap of 20' is either the utterance of a rogue who is capable of 15 on a good day or someone incapable of anything better than 40, or an egotist who likes to say 20 when he is really 24.

The mutterings get loudest as the 26 handicapper goes up to collect the cup or the golf bag at the end of the day's match. Other shades of mutter greet the success of the 4 handicap bighead who has actually played to it.

It is a fraught subject.

GOLF HUMOUR

Because humour comes hard to the golfer – a miserable wretch at the best of times – golf stories tend to be slightly sick. There are very few of the classic ones that do not mention, or at last hint at, death or destruction. As the same golf stories are told all over the world, it would be just as well if you knew the half-dozen or so basic ones so that you can stop other golfers from telling them – which they will do at the least provocation. Most classic golf stories concern dedication to 'the game'.

(1) Golf Pro: 'Keep a firm grip on the club, fingers overlapping and pointing down. Keep your head still and your eye on the ball. Now hit it smoothly...' Golfer hits the ball hard but laterally and it flies over the fence and into the adjoining road where it hits a motor-cyclist on the head. The motor-cyclist swerves towards a car and ends up in the ditch. The car swerves to avoid him and heads towards an oncoming bus which veers to the other side of the road and turns over. A lorry coming the other way runs into the back of the car and pushes it through the fence. Golfer (clearly in great distress): 'What shall I do? What shall I do?' Golf Pro: 'You must keep your right elbow closer to your side as you come through.'

(2) Three golfers go out for their weekly game. On the second green one of them has a heart attack and drops down dead. Later in the club house the secretary comes up to the others (who are having a drink to recover) and offers his condolences: 'I am so sorry. Your game must have been completely ruined!' 'No,' replies one of them, 'but it was a bit of a bind having to carry him round for the last sixteen holes.'

(3) A game is about to tee off at the first green when a funeral cortège passes on the nearby road. One of the golfers removes his cap and stands silent as it passes. 'Bill, I didn't know you were so religious,' says the other. 'I'm not usually,' said Bill, 'but it *was* my wife.'

(4) A golfer falls into the lake and cries out to his caddy: 'Help, help – I'm drowning!' 'Don't you worry, sir,' says the caddie, 'you won't drown. You never keep your head down long enough for that.'

(5) Lady passenger in car discovers some golf tees in the pocket. 'What are those for?' she asks. 'They are,' he replies, 'to rest your balls on when driving.'

(6) Golfer to caddie: 'Golf is a funny game!'
Caddie to golfer: 'It wasn't meant to be.'

It is up to the bluffing golfer to find one or two jokes that at least have the asset of not being one of those. A good joke, told at the right time, e.g. just before starting, when the opponent is at his most twitchy, might be worth several strokes on the first half. Most golf jokes are reserved however, as a means of alleviating the unremitting gloom of the average club-house.

GOLF LITERATURE

There are basically two kinds of books on golf – Instructional and Inspirational. The former should be pressed upon all those with whom you are likely to play. As Henry Longhurst once said, there is little to be learned from books of instruction by the great professionals. They just don't know what it feels like to be you. Try to do all the things they recommend and you will end up in hospital or on a psychiatrist's couch. So shower your golfing friends with books like *Sixty Easy Ways to Improve Your Swing*, and *Golfing Made Easy* because nothing will put them off their game more thoroughly. Our friend Alf has a roomful of books on how to play golf. He had to make himself a pair of library steps the other day so that he could reach the top ones. He fell off them and was unable to play for a fortnight. He reads a fresh one each week and avidly follows the instructional strip cartoons in the Sunday papers. Each week he gets a little more confused. For Christmas we are sending him *Putting Made Practical*.

The Inspirational books, on the other hand, while not actually doing anything for your game do nothing much to harm it either. They simply keep the golfer at it. The Inspirational literature of Golf is second only to that on Cricket. The twenty thousand volumes with titles like *The Golfer's Bumper Bedside Book*, the cosy essays written in an alcoholic haze by well-loved commentators, the ghosted autobiographies of the great, these are what bring us back to the rolling fairways each week. The gap between that which is remembered in tranquility and the actuality is immense. Most golf matches are really very prosaic but the memories of them are wreathed in poetry, human conflict and calculated exaggeration. They are full of reminiscences of how Archie Compton beat Walter Hagen in 1928, which don't do a lot for our golf but give us a totally unreasonable degree of inspiration. If Hagen was not daunted by this bunker – then nor are we.

Assiduous study of golfing literature is essential to the bluffer. All you need do is extract some dozen or so facts from it to be well armed. When your nervous opponent defends his action by reference to the style of Hogan you may then remind him that Varden did just the opposite. Indecision immediately creeps in.

A PURPLE PATCH

What golfer has not stepped out onto some glorious golf course on a sunny morning in early summer, the bogwort worting beneath his feet, the larks improvising overhead on a theme by Vaughan Williams, the air like a whiff of newly baked bread. Suppose, to lend fantasy to mere euphoria, that it is one of those heaven-planned courses like St. Enodoc in North Cornwall where the back half is a constant visual flirtation with the Camel estuary and the sparkling Atlantic beyond and where many of the bunkers are not crafty little man-made pits but whole sand-dunes fit for giants to play in. One green, nestling in a valley with a stream behind Bray Hill, is a sort of natural extension of that tiny church in whose graveyard the golfing spirit of Betjeman lies. But equally well, suppose it is a course carved out of the Surrey woodlands or the Yorkshire moors or the Scottish highlands; or it runs through the evergreen glades of Florida or up the pebbled coast of California; or it lies in postcard perfection, graced by every fellow comfort, in Portugal or Spain; or it is simply a bit of the Australian outback or the African veld. On crisp clear mornings each of these courses made for man's delight are simply good to be upon; they challenge you to a game. The rabbits scud, the magpies scrirch, the vultures swing to and fro overhead.

The club house flag flaps lazily. The irons in their head-down ranks in the golf-bag seem sharp and ready for the fray. The golfer's hands clasp naturally in an easy practice grip. The newly unwrapped golf ball is as white and shining as a toothpaste ad. One almost hears the distant roar of applause as the ball bounds onto the baize-like green and clips the pin. This is what it's all about.

Isn't it?

GLOSSARY

Address – A good address is considered essential to golf. Like, for instance, '18 Fairway Drive, Lytham St. Annes' or 'The Last Bunker, Wentworth Way' or 'Link's View, Westward Ho!' There is also the more technical meaning of shaping up to the ball. Once you have wiggled the head once or twice, shifted your feet, twitched your bottom, got into an approximate position, waggled the club and brought the head to the ground, you are deemed to have addressed the ball. Sort of said 'hello' to it. If after that you fall over backwards or the ball does, you are deemed to have made a shot.

Air-shot – This is when the golfer misses the ball altogether, which can be a better thing to do than catching it a whack on the side. The people he is playing will deem it a miss and add a point to his score. The player declares it a practice shot and a bitter argument ensues.

As it lies – Playing the ball from the place where it has by the laws of nature come to rest which, of course, is nearly always in a small hole or behind an obstruction. This difficulty is got over by a general agreement to play to 'winter rules' which means that the ball can be picked up and cleaned and replaced on any convenient small mound. Winter rules have been known to extend from the beginning of Autumn to the end of Spring.

Baffy – Ancient name for a No. 4 wood. Even experienced caddies can be put down by a request for a 'baffy'.

Balls – Correct response to opponent who suggests that you inadvertently touched the ball in addressing it and therefore should lose a stroke.

Birdie – A term denoting a hole score of one under par. Ornithological origins uncertain.

Blaster – Type of stroke used by Alf when in any sort of hazard. Or an early sand wedge.

Bogey – Taking more strokes on a hole than par – bogey-one, bogey-two, and so on. Called a bogey because all golfers are haunted by the thought of it.

Brassie – An archaic name applied to the No. 2 wood; or to a lady player who cuts in and holds up a men's game.

Bunker – A hole full of sand, half-bricks and an occasional poisonous snake, with a deep overhanging face on the side nearest the green, in which 25 per cent of golf-shots end up. When playing a ball in a bunker the head of the club must not touch the sand prior to the shot. Your opponents will be watching carefully for this. In the USA they are called traps.

Caddie – To use a caddie is a great mark of distinction. Not so much that you can afford one but that you play well enough not to be put off by his wrong advice and/or disbelief in your abilities.

Cleek – Either (a) a shallow-faced iron corresponding to the modern No. 2, or (b) the lot that run the golf club and think they own it.

Dog leg – A hole (fairway) which bends right or left and offers the player the awful temptation of trying to cut the corner (usually with disastrous results) or going round the safe way. A lot of golfers' troubles stem from their dog legs.

Draw – Either (a) a shot deliberately played so that it moves out to the right and then in again towards its destination (the opposite of *Fade*); (b) the amateur's description of what his opponent describes as a *Hook*.

56

Driver, Driving-off – The Driver is a wooden club with the straightest of faces, also known as a No. 1. Meant to send the ball the maximum distance, it is also the one most likely to send it in the wrong direction or into the ground, so most amateurs prefer to use a No. 2 or 3. Many drive-off with an iron, so the two terms are not intimately connected.

Eagle – A score for a hole that is two less than par. It is called an eagle because it is a very rare bird.

Fade – Either (a) a shot deliberately played so that it moves out to the left and then in again toward its destination (the opposite of *Draw*); (b) the amateur's description of what a more critical person would describe as a *Slice*; or (c) what the elderly and overweight golfer starts to do round about the 14th on a hot day.

Fairway – The parts of the course where anything that goes wrong is the golfer's own fault.

Fluff – An excessively feeble shot. Or a right mess.

Fore! – A warning cry, either uttered just too late to prevent an insurance claim; or too early in the over-optimistic expectation that the ball will travel far enough to hit a distant group of players.

Gimmie – A putt of a length which the player deems his opponent could not possibly miss and therefore need not attempt. There is no fixed length and a great deal of difference between what is expected (about two or three feet) and what is conceded (about two or three inches). After a gimmie, for some inexplicable reason, most players still have a go and often miss, though they still claim to have won the hole, which greatly upsets their opponent.

Green – An area of smooth grass with a hole in the bumpy bit.

Ground under repair – Condition of those parts of the course where some golfer had a spot of bother.

Hazard – Standing anywhere within the arc of 180 degrees (and even more on windy days) in front of a rank amateur as he takes a shot. Any deliberately devised trap for the unwary.

Holed out – A term meaning that the ball has gone in.

Hook – A shot that veers right then goes wildly out to the left. Players more commonly refer to it as *Draw*.

Iron – Originally this was a special name for a metal headed club with a fairly straight face, something between a cleek and a mashie – what might now be referred to as a No. 3. Today the term 'iron' is employed to categorise all metal-headed clubs that are not woods (many of which are now confusingly made of metal). It was the Duke of Wellington, who favoured this sort of club rather than a wood, who first made it popular and was thenceforth familiarly known at his Club as the 'iron Duke'.

Jigger – Long obsolete iron with a narrow blade. Today's equivalent would be a No. 4 iron. So-called from the persistent remark made by one famous old-Etonian golfer whenever he used it and observed the result 'well, I'll be jiggered'. While your opponent is trying to work out what a jigger is, his mind can appreciably wander from the game.

Knoll – cf. *Oxford Dictionary* – 'a small eminence of more or less rounded form', i.e. an elderly golfer.

Lie – Either where the ball has come to rest or where the player claims that it came to rest.

Lost ball – What a ball is deemed to be if it disappears in the undergrowth and is not found within five minutes. Ten with some of the uncivilized lot you get on golf courses today. A ball about to be played by Alf could almost certainly be pre-designated a lost ball. Alf is the original person involved in the duologue: 'Why do you keep using a new ball when you are only going to lose it. Why don't you use an old one?' Alf: 'Because I've never had an old one.' (Sigh.)

Mashie – An iron club. In its heyday, hickory-shafted, it became the golfer's favourite iron; some using it for practically everything. Even when it became more prosaically known as a No. 5 iron. There was also a spade mashie, nearer to a No. 6, and a mashie-niblick which was more like a No. 7.

Middling – Far from being rather average, middling in golf is the amateur's ambition. If he middles the ball horizontally there is a fair chance that it will go quite a long way, and if he middles it perpendicularly it will probably go straight. If he manages both at the same time the result (far from being middling, in the general sense) is nothing short of miraculous.

Niblick – A golf club with a very sloping face (now generally referred to as a No. 9 iron) introduced by Lord Niblick of Strathshaven in 1862. It was a mashie when he started the game but then he was a violent man. When asked at the end of a round 'What do you call that thing?' he replied, rather rudely, 'Call it a ruddy niblick if you like!'

Par – The score per hole that is considered reasonably within the reach of an ordinary adult. The amateur is very pleased with it but the professional is displeased at not having got a birdie of some kind. Golfers, unlike most, generally feel good if they are under par.

Playing through – It is considered polite, when looking for a lost ball or otherwise bringing play to a halt, to allow those behind on the fairway to play through. For some reason there is a 75 per cent chance that those doing so will play duff shots and possibly end up in a similar position. There is then much confusion and ill-feeling.

Putting – What ought to be the easiest part of golf, when the ball is lying on the close-cropped grass of the green and only needs a well-judged shot to end up in the hole. Unfortunately it is where most hearts are broken when for example one has arrived on the green for three and then takes another three to get down. There are endless anguished conversations about 'borrows', 'line', and much self-analysis. Some players use the putter off the green, in which case it is not called a putter but a Texas wedge.

Ray, Ted – British golfer (1877-1947). Asked for advice on how to hit the ball farther, he replied: 'Hit it a bloody sight harder!' Worth a special entry for this.

Scratch player – A person not to be spoken to by the ordinary golfer until they have spoken first.

Shanking – A dreaded mishap that afflicts golfers who stand too near their balls.

Slice – A shot that goes out to the left in a great arc and ends up on the right of the fairway. Most slicers refer to their mishaps as *Fade*.

Spoon – A wooden headed club with a sloping face (equivalent of the modern No. 3 wood).

Stableford – A crafty way of scoring a game of golf, invented in 1932 by a Dr Frank B. Stableford. It is really for the benefit of the bad golfer who may go a whole round without winning a single hole. In

Stableford scoring you get 2 points for a par and even 1 for a one-over bogey; 3 points for a birdie; 4 for an eagle, and so on, after allowing for points given according to handicap. So the bluffing golfer simply says he scored 23 and needs offer no further details. No point in revealing that he scored nothing at all on several holes, cheated slightly and lost three balls.

Stance – An odd and unnatural way of standing recommended by teaching pros.

Tee – Either the area, marked by various white, yellow or red plastic cones (or, in some clubs, big plastic golfballs) from whence one begins to assault each hole; or a small peg with a recessed top made of wood or plastic (often with 'Invest with the Halifax' or some such ill-timed exhortation written on it) on which the ball is placed, thus elevating it from the ground, before driving off (see *Driver*). Hence 'tee-hee' an expression used by those watching when somebody misses the ball.

Topping – Not used in golf in the sense that P. G. Wodehouse might have used – 'absolutely topping, Jeeves', or 'a topping wheeze' – nor that which is used by pastry cooks. In golf it means hitting the ball on its top bit rather than in the middle (where you should) so that it scuttles along the ground before coming to rest behind a *knoll*.

Twitch – Putter's disease. Said to be incurable except by regular injections of alcohol.

Wedge – A golfer with a very sloping face.

Woods – Wooden-headed clubs, increasingly made of metal. Now, like irons, they have anonymous numbers which used to be (equivalents) No. 1 – driver; No. 2 – brassie; No. 3 – spoon; No. 4 – baffy; No. 5 – baffier. Nowadays the repertoire has been increased, ranging up to a No. 8.

THE AUTHOR

Peter Gammond's qualifications to write a book about Golf could quite easily be questioned. His evasive answer is that anyone who has lived is entitled to write a novel about it. The present book, as you will have discovered, is not, in any case, a technical treatise. How could anyone who is incapable of stringing more than three good shots together (and those on different holes) embark on that anyway. But it is, so the author claims, a philosophical view of golf expressing thoughts which he sincerely believes he shares with thousands of others who have suffered with him.

Born not far from a golf course, he did not, in fact, strike his first ball in earnest until invited to play in Oxford in 1943. The very first ball he hit went straight down the fairway and he decided there and then to take up the game. The second, third and subsequent hits made him reverse this decision; and it was not until 1962 that he again approached Golf, having by that time been forced to give up more active sports such as Darts and Shove-halfpenny. He joined a Surrey golf club that year along with his friend Alf. It was only Alf's constant encouragement (by always playing rather worse than he did) that has kept him at the game ever since. Peter Gammond, F.R.S.G.R., S.H.A.G.S* lives in a house but keeps his golf clubs in the garden shed in the hope that one day someone will come and pinch them. He can then collect the insurance money and retire from the game.

* Fellow of the Royal Society of Golfing Rabbits, Member of the Surrey & Hounslow Ambulatory Golfing Society.